Working With Animals

Wild Careers!

Working With Animals

PART OF THE SEAWORLD EDUCATION SERIES

Research/Writing/Layout/Editing
Loran Wlodarski

Technical Advisors
Brad Andrews
Tom Goff
Jerry Goldsmith
Thad Lacinak
Daniel K. Odell (Hubbs-SeaWorld
    Research Institute)
John Kerivan
Mike Scarpuzzi
Mike Shaw
Chuck Tompkins

Editorial Staff
Judith Coats
Dennis Jones
Deborah Nuzzolo
Donna Parham
Jody Rake

Education Directors
Hollis J. Gillespie
Kimberly Laska
John Lowe
Joy L. Wolf

Photos
Mike Aguilera
Bob Couey
Bob French
Richmond Gibbs
Chris Gotshall
Julio Lopez
Carol Swain
Busch Gardens Tampa Bay
    Photo Department
SeaWorld Orlando
    Photo Department
SeaWorld San Diego
    Photo Department

Cover: A false killer whale (*Pseudorca crassidens*) interacts with a SeaWorld trainer.
Title page: SeaWorld and Busch Gardens Animal Ambassador Julie Scardina feeds
a group of manatees (*Trichechus manatus latirostris*).
Contents page: Newly hatched scarlet macaw chicks (*Ara macao*) receive
around-the-clock care by experts at SeaWorld and Busch Gardens.
Page 1: Senior trainer Kathleen Gass works with an African fish eagle (*Haliaeetus vocifer*).
Pages 48–49: Camp SeaWorld students meet Indy, a common green iguana
(*Iguana iguana*).
Pages 70–71: "Trainer for a Day" participants at SeaWorld Orlando get an up-close
look at how false killer whales are weighed.
Page 82: Raising newly hatched penguin chicks (Family Speniscidae) can be a handful.
Page 84: An Asian small-clawed otter is weighed during its exam.
Page 85: Senior trainer Eric Lang poses with an Asian small-clawed otter (*Aonyx cinerea*).
Page 86: Aquarist Laura Simmons examines shark eggs to check on their development.
Page 87: *Wild Careers!* author Loran Wlodarski introduces a young Camp SeaWorld
participant to a domesticated rabbit (Family Leporidae).

©2006 SeaWorld Inc. All Rights Reserved.

Published by the SeaWorld Education Department
7007 SeaWorld Drive, Orlando, Florida 32821

ISBN 1–893698–08–4
Printed in the United States of America

Contents

A Career That's Really Wild

"A man on a horse is spiritually as well as physically bigger than a man on foot."

John Steinbeck

*H*umans *Caring for Animals*

Are you wild about animals? Can you turn your love of animals into a career? Hundreds of jobs involve working with animals. Some involve direct contact with animals and some do not.

Why do people who work with animals do what they do? We asked them. Most told us that their passion began with a visit to a zoo or oceanarium. Zoos and aquariums hold many job opportunities for animal lovers. SeaWorld and Busch Gardens Adventure Parks employ more than 600 animal care professionals. And your opportunities are not limited to zoos. Ranches, laboratories, and field stations also offer careers in animal care.

Throughout history, people have relied on animals. Farmers and ranchers have raised sheep, cattle, goats, and horses for about 5,000 years. More than 9,000 years ago, our ancestors kept dogs for companionship, protection, and hunting.

Our partnership with animals has profoundly changed human cultures. Domesticating horses made it possible for people to travel great distances. Horses made exploration and trade possible. And they gave warriors an advantage on the battlefield.

People have kept collections of animals for thousands of years. The earliest zoos were privately owned animal collections that weren't open to the public. Such zoos showcased the wealth and prestige of the noble classes.

Historians think that the ancient Greeks were the first to open zoos to the public. These zoos were places where students could learn about animal and plant life. In the late 1400s, European explorers brought strange, exotic creatures home from their travels. Animal collections grew. The first modern zoo began as a private collection in Vienna, Austria. It was transformed into a public facility in 1765. With modern zoos came the need for animal care professionals.

Horses (*Equus caballus*) shaped the growth of human culture as few animals have. Their proper care and breeding created the need for some of the earliest animal care specialists and veterinarians.

Careers that put humans in direct contact with animals are some of the most fascinating jobs on earth. Yet zoo visitors observe very little of the daily routines of animal care professionals. Most of their work goes on behind the scenes.

In the animal care field, career requirements and responsibilities vary by job. Preparation and training for some of these careers is rigorous and time-consuming. As members of the American Zoo and Aquarium Association (AZA) and the Alliance of Marine Mammal Parks and Aquariums (AMMPA), SeaWorld and Busch Gardens adhere to the highest standards of animal care. This book profiles various animal-related careers at Busch Gardens, Discovery Cove, and SeaWorld Adventure Parks. After reading this book, you'll discover that there are many diverse career possibilities for people who want to work with animals.

Animal training positions are highly sought after, but there are many other animal career opportunities at zoos.

The animal care staff rescues and rehabilitates marine mammals such as manatees.

Animal Training

An animal trainer's job is one of the most visible and desired jobs in a zoological park. At SeaWorld and Busch Gardens parks, animal trainers work with parrots and other birds, sea lions, walruses, otters, whales, and dolphins. Trainers must be ready and willing to work with any animal species.

Animal training is one of the most rigorous as well as rewarding fields in a zoological park. Some of their duties include...

- maintaining the physical, mental and emotional well-being of the animals
- conducting training sessions with animals
- developing training techniques
- preparing and distributing food
- exercising the animals
- assisting the veterinarians with medical examinations
- performing in public shows
- keeping the animal habitats and show areas clean and safe
- observing animals and documenting their behavior
- keeping health and diet records

Trainers present animal shows for large audiences every day. They must deliver a lively and enthusiastic presentation each time. Animal trainers must maintain a high level of physical fitness to safely perform their duties. Applicants can expect a rigorous swim test and must be able to lift and carry at least 22.7 kg (50 lb.). They also must have a great deal of patience and consistency. Gaining the trust of new animals and shaping show behaviors require years of hard work and commitment.

Animal trainers may be scheduled to work at any time and day of the week. They often work outdoors in all types of weather. Sometimes they are required to travel and to assist in transporting animals.

Opportunities for animal trainers are very limited. For every opening there may be dozens of qualified applicants. But anyone with the right experience and abilities can be an animal trainer. Preparation for the job may begin years before you apply.

Very few colleges offer an animal training degree. But other types of college degrees and courses are helpful when preparing for an animal training career. Many animal trainers have a degree in animal behavior, psychology, or zoology. To help them be good performers, they may choose an educational background in drama or communications. Trainers are also required to be CPR and first aid-certified, and most must be scuba-trained as well.

While the right education is a good place to start, first-hand animal experience is essential. Many animal trainers got their start volunteering their time behind the scenes at a zoo or veterinary hospital. Others had experience handling horses or exotic birds. Establishing a history of animal care and handling gives many future animal trainers an edge.

A false killer whale has its teeth examined by a SeaWorld trainer.

At SeaWorld, it takes advanced swimming skills and years of training before an animal trainer can get in the water with a killer whale (*Orcinus orca*).

Chuck Cureau
Senior Animal Trainer
SeaWorld San Antonio

1. *What's the most exciting part of your job?*
Sharing SeaWorld's animals with our
guests is my favorite job responsibility.
I absolutely love allowing people to get
up close with the animals and to get
a little taste of what I do on a daily basis.

2. *What do you want to get involved with next?*
I want to increase my involvement in media-related animal
presentations. I've been very fortunate to have represented
SeaWorld and Busch Gardens in several TV shows and news
releases, and hope to continue doing this on a larger scale.

3. *What's your most unforgettable moment on the job?*
Seeing animals born are among my most memorable
experiences. Births are the result of excellent animal care and
training, state-of-the-art facilities, and teamwork among several
SeaWorld departments. Births are a testament to the excellent
work done by our company, and I'm proud to be a part of that.

4. *What advice do you have for young people who would like to
do what you do?*
Learn as much about animals as possible, perfect your
swimming skills, learn the fundamentals of behavioral
psychology, and develop good communication and
teamwork skills.

5. *What school subjects would be helpful for your field of work?*
Behavioral psychology, zoology, and general biology are all
subjects that will prepare an individual for a career as an animal
trainer. Animal trainers must also be proficient in math, writing,
and public speaking.

6. *What are your favorite books related to your field of work?*
I enjoy reading articles about animal training that are published
in the International Marine Animal Training Association's
Soundings. A book that I reference regularly is *Behavioral
Modification in Applied Settings* by Alan Kazdin.

Animal Training Career Ladder

There are several career levels that a trainer can reach through experience and development. Most animal trainers start as an apprentice trainer, no matter how much time they may have spent training animals outside of SeaWorld or Busch Gardens. A lengthy apprenticeship acquaints new trainers with SeaWorld training methods and with the animals' individual personalities. Killer whale trainers may be on the job for two years or longer before entering the water with the huge animals.

Over time, apprentice trainers may become associate trainers, trainers, and senior trainers. Senior trainers perform in many of the park shows. They also help to acquaint new trainers to the animals and introduce apprentice trainers to the training concepts used by SeaWorld and Busch Gardens.

Management levels in the training department require years of experience as a senior trainer. The supervisor of animal training, for example, must have at least two years experience as a senior trainer. The supervisor of animal training oversees an entire show area. He or she also helps to develop new show behaviors and enrichment programs for animals in their care.

The vice president of animal training usually has at least ten years experience at SeaWorld, at least seven at a managerial level. In addition to overseeing the daily operations of the animal training

staff and animal collection, the vice president of animal training creates the goals and direction for the department. He or she also assists with the design of new animal habitats, attractions, and show areas.

A successful trainer must be patient. It may take years of effort to gain an animal's trust.

Animal Care/Animal Keeper

The animal care/animal keeper staff are responsible for the daily care of the park mammals. Mammals are a wide and diverse group that includes such animals as dolphins, sea lions, hippopotamuses, polar bears, porcupines, camels, and bats.

Some of their duties include...

- preparing and distributing food
- assisting the veterinarians with medical examinations
- keeping the animal habitats and show areas clean and safe
- observing animals and documenting their behavior
- keeping health and diet records
- conducting training sessions with some types of animals
- answering guest questions and speaking to educational groups

Busch Gardens Tampa Bay animal keepers look after camels (Family Camelidae) and many other mammals.

Experienced animal care keepers often rescue and rehabilitate ill, orphaned, or injured animals. SeaWorld has the most successful manatee rehabilitation program in the world, for example. Experts have successfully rescued, rehabilitated, and released more than 100 manatees to date.

Animal care keepers may work at any time and day of the week. They usually work outdoors in all types of weather. Sometimes they are required to travel and assist in transporting animals.

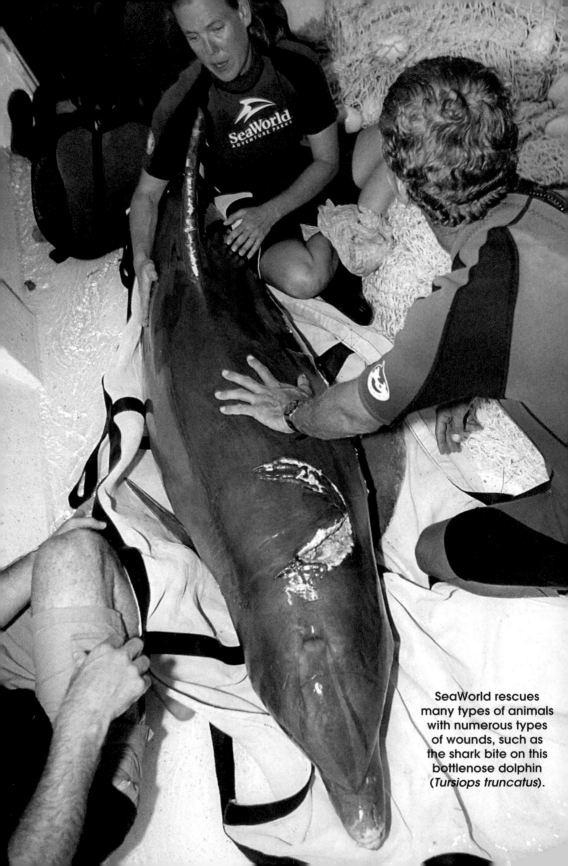

SeaWorld rescues many types of animals with numerous types of wounds, such as the shark bite on this bottlenose dolphin (*Tursiops truncatus*).

There are many potential hazards when it comes to rescuing large animals that are injured and frightened. Because of the risk involved, the animal care staff is trained on safety procedures, including scuba, CPR, first aid, and net safety courses. Heavy lifting is often involved in feeding mammals or rescuing large, stranded animals. Each keeper must be able to lift at least 13.6 kg (30 lb.) on a regular basis.

Many of the animals, although not featured in a show, may be trained in basic husbandry procedures. Animals are trained to relax and hold still while keepers examine them. This makes it easier to care for animals without causing them much stress.

Many animal care employees or keepers have a Bachelor's degree in biology or zoology. A college degree is preferred, but experience is helpful. Raising cattle, horses, goats, and other mammals can be of great benefit to a person thinking about a career caring for park mammals. Volunteering at veterinary hospitals, animal shelters, pet stores, or ranches are helpful as well.

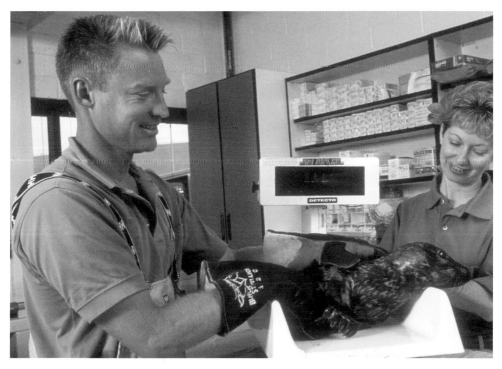

Animals at SeaWorld and Busch Gardens receive consistent medical check-ups. Here two animal keepers weigh a harbor seal (Phoca vitulina) pup.

Coffy Bennis
Primate Keeper, Myombe Reserve
Busch Gardens Tampa Bay

1. *What's the most exciting part of your job?*
   It's exciting to build relationships with the animals I care for, especially with great apes. Earning their trust can be a very long and difficult process. But, in the end, when an animal who has been hesitant of you finally shows they trust you it is one of the most rewarding experiences in the world.

2. *What do you want to get involved with next?*
   I would like to return to working with great apes in the wild, be it orangutans in Borneo or chimpanzees in Africa. My experience in Uganda and Kenya with the Jane Goodall Institute working with chimpanzees has been a true highlight in my life.

3. *What's your most unforgettable moment on the job?*
   Chimpanzees are incredible politicians, and this became evident during a recent introduction of two new chimps at Busch Gardens. We watched alliances being torn in two, only to be rebuilt seconds later. It was amazing to see how intelligent they are and watch the social hierarchy being restructured right in front of our eyes.

4. *What advice do you have for young people who would like to do what you do?*
   Learn what type of animals you would like to work with the most and plan a trip to see those animals in the wild. I decided to travel to Africa to see chimps in the wild, and was lucky enough to land a position with the Jane Goodall Institute.

5. *What school subjects would be helpful for your field of work?*
   I am majoring in anthropology, which focuses on primate behavior and evolution. If you believe you'd like to work with primates, this is a good subject to study. Biology, of course, is a very broad and useful subject.

6. *What are your favorite books related to your field of work?*
   Next of Kin by Roger Fouts
   Gorillas in the Mist by Dian Fossey
   Reflections of Eden by Dr. Birute Galdikas
   Through a Window and *In the Shadow of Man* by Jane Goodall

Animal Care Career Ladder

Most people begin their career in the animal care department as a husbandry assistant. This introductory position enables the employee to get familiar with the park and its mammals. A husbandry assistant spends most of this or her time preparing and distributing food. A husbandry assistant also learns how to properly feed and care for the park's mammals. With experience, a husbandry assistant can advance to other levels including animal care specialist trainees, animal care specialists, senior animal care specialists, and supervisors of mammals.

The department receives its overall vision and direction from the curator of mammals. The curator of mammals is primarily responsible for the long-range management of the animal care department and its daily operations. Curators use their in-depth knowledge of mammals to develop and manage breeding programs. This includes creating and maintaining studbooks for long-term breeding programs. The curator is also responsible for the development and design of new animal habitats and attractions. He or she works with contractors during the construction process.

In addition, the curator of mammals may need to travel for extended periods to meet with other professionals, and when transporting animals.

A young kudu (*Tragelaphus imberbis*) is bottle fed in front of an enthusiastic crowd.

Animal trainers in marine life parks usually are required to have advanced swimming skills.

*S*wimming Skills

How well can you swim? This is a serious question to consider before applying for some of the animal-related positions at marine life parks. Animal trainers, for example, spend a lot of time in the water. Animal rescuers may need to plunge into murky, unfamiliar waters. They must have first aid training and advanced swimming skills to be prepared for any situation.

At SeaWorld, many applicants must complete a rigorous swim test before they are even interviewed for a position. The SeaWorld swim test is done in a cold, saltwater stadium pool.

Participants can wear a bathing suit or wet suit, but scuba equipment and weight belts are not permitted.

Part of the test is a 67-m (220-ft.) free style swim. The participant must swim at least half the distance under water. Participants also perform a 7.3-m (24-ft.) free dive to retrieve a small weight and bring it to the surface.

Afterward, participants come out of the water onto the stage, where they are further tested by doing push-ups. Finally, participants speak into a microphone to test the clarity of their voice after the physical exertion.

Test requirements vary from one park to the next, but this is an example of what one might expect during a SeaWorld swim test.

Aquarium

Members of the aquarium department are responsible for one of the largest and most varied groups of park animals. In addition to caring for fishes, they also manage invertebrates, including sea stars, sea urchins, jellyfishes, and snails, among others. Amphibians and reptiles, including sea turtles and alligators, often fall under their care and responsibility as well. Large reptile and amphibian collections, such as those at Busch Gardens Tampa Bay, are managed by a herpetology department.

Some of their duties include...

- maintaining all park aquariums and habitats
- preparing and distributing food
- assisting the veterinarians with medical examinations
- keeping the animal habitats areas clean and safe
- observing animals and documenting their behavior
- keeping health and diet records
- answering guest questions and speaking to educational groups

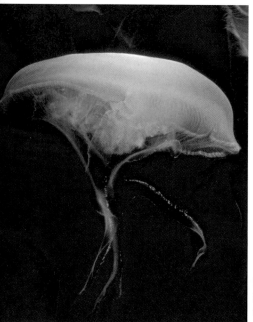

The aquarium department rescues and rehabilitates animals such as sea turtles. In fact, SeaWorld has one of the best facilities in the world for the rescue and rehabilitation of endangered and threatened sea turtles. There is a lot of heavy lifting involved when an animal is rescued, so aquarists must be able to regularly lift at least 22.7 kg (50 lb.).

In addition to fish, the aquarium staff cares for amphibians, reptiles, and invertebrates such as this jellyfish (Class Scyphozoa).

Aquarists at SeaWorld Orlando prepare to release a rehabilitated loggerhead sea turtle (*Caretta caretta*).

Aquarium systems can be complex. Experience caring for aquatic animals is quite helpful. Volunteering at local zoos and aquariums, working in a pet store, or building and maintaining a home aquariums are great ways to gain experience. Aquarists may have to build a new system or monitor water quality. Many have an understanding of basic chemistry and plumbing skills.

Aquariums are becoming increasingly popular for cities and private businesses. In response to demand for quality aquarists, several colleges are offering degrees in marine sciences and aquarium sciences (see pages 78–79 for more details). Aquarists must have at least an Associate's degree. Scuba certification is required to work in the aquarium department.

Aquarists often work outdoors in all types of weather and may be scheduled to work at any time and day of the week. Sometimes they are required to travel and to assist in transporting animals, or to rescue and release animals such as sea turtles.

An aquarist must clean fish habitats, which may contain hundreds of thousands of liters of water, on a daily basis.

Gary Violetta
Curator of Fishes
SeaWorld Orlando

1. *What's the most exciting part of your job?*
The most exciting part of my job is building new habitats, starting from the conceptual stage through the final completion. The best part of this is hearing all the great comments from the park guests about the aquarium or the animals on display.

2. *What do you want to get involved with next?*
The next step for the aquarium department is to become more involved in the reproduction of certain targeted animals. These animals include sharks, rays, jellyfish, and a few fish.

3. *What's your most unforgettable moment on the job?*
My most memorable experience was the first time I helped rescue a whale shark that was stranded on a sandbar. To be that close to such magnificent creature and being one of a dozen people helping push it off the sandbar was a remarkable experience.

4. *What advice do you have for young people who would like to do what you do?*
I recommend graduating from college with a BS in marine science or a similar field and getting scuba certified. I would also do something special to set myself apart from other individuals who are trying to break into this field, such as volunteering in the college marine lab or working at a pet store.

5. *What school subjects would be helpful for your field of work?*
Along with basic biology, chemistry, and marine biology courses, I would look for any aquatic oriented classes such as limnology and algology. Also, anatomy, environmental physiology, and parasitology. And, again, any course work or independent study that will give you the edge over other people.

6. *What are your favorite books related to your field of work?*
The Book of Sharks by Richard Ellis
Fish and Invertebrate Culture and Captive Seawater Systems by Steven Spotte
The Marine Aquarium Reference by Martin Moe, Jr.

Aquarium Department Career Ladder

Many people begin their career in the aquarium department as a husbandry assistant. This introductory position enables the new aquarist to get familiar with the park and its animals. A husbandry assistant spends most of his or her time preparing and distributing food. A husbandry assistant also learns how to properly feed and care for fish, invertebrates, and other aquarium animals. With experience, a husbandry assistant can advance to other levels including aquarist trainees, senior aquarists, assistant supervisors, supervisors assistant curators, and curator of fishes.

The curator of fishes creates the long-range goals and manages the aquarium department. The curator acquires new animals, monitors animal diets, and is responsible for all scientific research programs of the department. The curator also helps to design new animal exhibits. One of the biggest challenges for the curator of fishes involves the development of innovative water filtration processes.

The curator of fishes needs to have approximately ten years experience, seven of which are at a managerial level. Some other key requirements include a Bachelor's degree in biological sciences plus scuba certification.

Aquarists work with a great variety of animal life.

Aviculture

A viculture literally means "the culture of birds," or the care, housing, and feeding of birds. Aviculturists care for a park's bird collection, from penguins to macaws, ostriches to hummingbirds.

An aviculturist may care for a bird long before it hatches.

Some of their duties include...

- maintaining all bird habitats
- preparing and distributing food
- assisting the veterinarians with medical examinations
- keeping the animal habitats areas clean and safe
- observing animals and documenting their behavior
- keeping health and diet records
- answering guest questions and speaking to educational groups

SeaWorld and Busch Gardens continue to be leaders in bird breeding programs. Highly endangered species such as white-winged wood ducks (*Cairina scutulata*) and Hawaiian nene geese (*Branta sandvicensis*) breed at SeaWorld and Busch Gardens. Aviculturists often raise young hatchlings. This requires an enormous amount of time because most chicks must be fed frequently.

An aviculturist usually has an Associate's or Bachelor's degree. To care for aquatic birds such as penguins, scuba certification is needed. Experience working with animals at another zoological park, veterinary hospital, animal shelter, pet store, or ranch is essential in this field. Many local bird organizations and public zoos that house birds usually need volunteers.

Aviculturists may be required to work at any time and day of the week. Their work is done outdoors in all types of weather. Aviculturists may be needed for 24-hour care of hatchlings or critically injured birds such as pelicans and cranes. Sometimes they need to travel in order to transport, rescue, or release birds.

The aviculture department has helped to rescue, rehabilitate, and release hundreds of birds including pelicans (Family Pelecanidae).

Courtney Harris
Aviculturist
Discovery Cove Orlando

1. *What's the most exciting part of your job?*
   The relationship that I have developed with each of the birds is truly rewarding. It takes time and dedication to establish this trust and when it evolves, it is amazing.

2. *What do you want to get involved with next?*
   I feel as if I'm constantly getting involved in new things with my position. It's definitely a constant learning process involving new species of birds, behaviors, and procedures. I'd like to continue this learning curve with birds, as well as becoming exposed to different species through cross training with other departments.

3. *What's your most unforgettable moment on the job?*
   Opening day at Discovery Cove was truly unforgettable. It was the time that our aviculture staff could relish in all the work that we had put into shaping the birds behaviors up to this point. Just to see the reactions from the guests as they enjoyed a once-in-a-lifetime experience was highly rewarding.

4. *What advice do you have for young people who would like to do what you do?*
   My best advice would be to stay in school and to get as much experience as you can. This experience could range from becoming a docent at a zoo, working in a veterinary hospitals, pet stores, and so on. On-the- job training is great, but having the education behind it will teach you so much more.

5. *What school subjects would be helpful for your field of work?*
   Any science subjects are definitely beneficial, especially biology and chemistry. As you get into higher learning there are definitely some specific subjects that were very informative such as ornithology, mammalogy, animal behavior, and psychology.

6. *What are your favorite books related to your field of work?*
   Don't Shoot the Dog by Karen Pryor
   Ornithology by Frank B. Gill
   The Life of Birds by David Attenborough

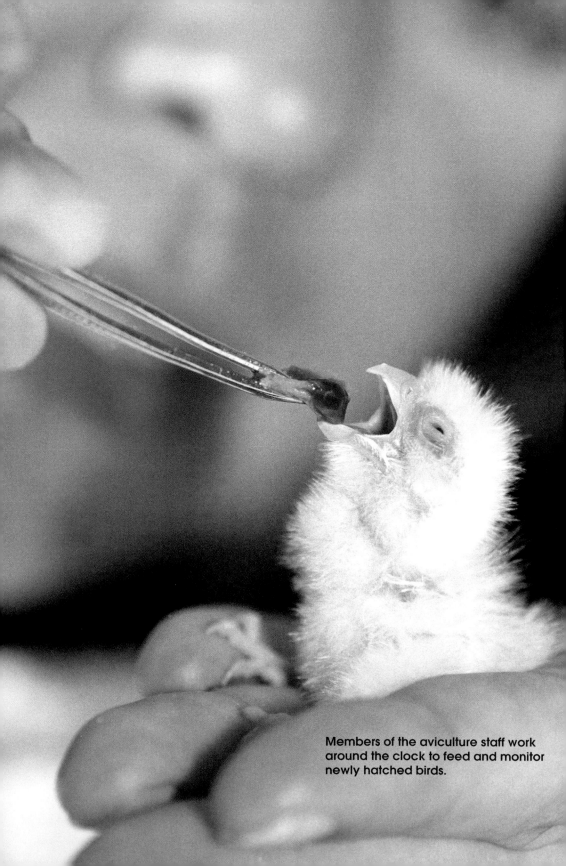

Members of the aviculture staff work around the clock to feed and monitor newly hatched birds.

Aviculture Department Career Ladder

Many people begin their career in the aviculture department as aviculture trainees. Aviculture trainees learn how to clean bird habitats and prepare bird diets. With experience, aviculture trainees can advance to other levels including aviculturists, senior aviculturists, supervisor of birds, and curator of birds.

The supervisor of birds oversees the daily operations of the aviculture department and helps train new staff. The supervisor of birds is also responsible for keeping records and for transporting birds.

The supervisor of birds usually has at least five years experience in the aviculture department. An Associate's or Bachelor's degree is also required, and in some cases, so is scuba certification.

The curator of birds is responsible for the long-range goals and daily operations of the aviculture department. Curators use their in-depth knowledge of birds to develop and manage breeding programs. They often work with other curators from across the country to create *Species Survival Plans* for certain types of birds. The curator of birds also helps develop new animal habitats and attractions, ensuring that plants and materials used for displays are safe for the birds.

Generally, a curator of birds has at least ten years experience, seven of which should be at a managerial level. The curator of birds is usually required to have a Bachelor's degree or equivalent in biological sciences.

Caring for penguins often requires working in chilly and wet conditions.

Veterinary Services

The accurate diagnosis of animal illnesses and injuries presents unique challenges. Often, the first (and sometimes only) sign that an animal may be ill or injured is a slight change in behavior. The veterinary services department uses laboratory testing and years of experience to treat animals.

Veterinary Technician

A veterinary technician primarily serves as an assistant to the staff veterinarian.

Some of his or her duties include...

- maintaining accurate medical records
- scheduling animal procedures such as physicals and surgeries
- collecting blood, urine, and stool samples
- setting up treatment and surgery rooms before operations
- maintaining and ordering medical equipment

The veterinary technician helps with surgical and medical procedures such as injections and X-rays. Because ill or injured animals are sometimes difficult to handle, veterinary technicians need good physical strength to assist in some procedures.

Before surgery to remove a fishing hook caught in its throat, a green sea turtle (*Chelonia mydas*) is given anesthetic gas.

A veterinary technician usually has spent considerable time working around animals. They are required to have an Animal Health Technician certification from an accredited institution or a medical technology degree. Veterinary technicians work with staff veterinarians, laboratory staff, and all of the animal services departments to ensure the health of park animals.

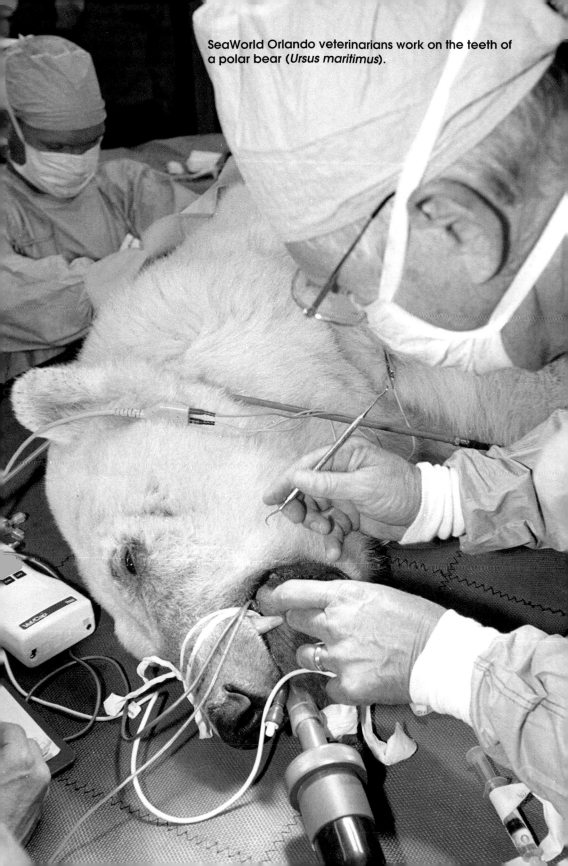

SeaWorld Orlando veterinarians work on the teeth of a polar bear (*Ursus maritimus*).

Clif Martel

Veterinary Technician
Busch Gardens Tampa Bay

1. *What's the most exciting part of your job?*
   I have the ability to work with every
   species at Busch Gardens, and the
   opportunity to make a positive
   contribution to the plight of many
   endangered animals.

2. *What do you want to get involved with next?*
   I'm interested in the administrative aspects of the zoological
   field, and I'm currently working on my Master's degree in
   business administration. I feel my experience in the hospital has
   given me a well-rounded view of the park, and would recommend
   this path for any career within the zoological field.

3. *What's your most unforgettable moment on the job?*
   Training a silverback gorilla to allow me to brush his teeth. I
   went through several toothbrushes before making any progress.

4. *What advice do you have for young people who would like to
   do what you do?*
   Gain as much experience working with animals as you can.
   Network, network, network. It is a very small world within the
   zoo community. Knowing people within the field is very helpful
   when it comes time to get a job.

5. *What school subjects would be helpful for your field of work?*
   While animal-related courses are obviously recommended,
   don't forget broad ranging courses. I have a Bachelor's degree
   in biology, with a concentration in genetics. I feel majoring in
   something other than animal sciences gives you a more rounded
   education that can later be applied to the field.

6. *What are your favorite books related to your field of work?*
   I have always loved *National Geographic* magazine, and would
   recommend it to anyone. You should be able to find a little
   something for everybody within it. There are also many good
   books on behavior modification; a good one to start with is
   Don't Shoot the Dog by Karen Pryor.

All animals at SeaWorld, Discovery Cove, and Busch Gardens get regular medical check-ups, including the sharks. Staff veterinarians assist in these procedures.

Staff Veterinarian

Staff veterinarians are responsible for all animal medical programs and procedures. This includes collecting blood and urine samples, conducting physical exams, treating injuries, and performing surgery and sonograms. Veterinarians make regular rounds and meet with all animal services staff to monitor the health of the animals.

Some of their duties include...

- maintaining the health and well-being of the park animals
- overseeing and enhancing animal nutrition programs
- collecting blood, urine and stool samples
- performing research projects
- making professional presentations at meetings
- serving on state and federal conservation committees

In their senior year, veterinary students can take part in an "externship" at a zoological park. After veterinary school, graduates may spend one to four years as an intern or two years in a residency position.

As part of its overall physical exam, a killer whale has been trained to cooperate with trainers so that X-rays can be taken of its teeth. Staff veterinarians develop preventive health care programs to keep park animals fit and strong.

Veterinarians usually have a Bachelor's degree in biological sciences or chemistry, and a Doctorate of Veterinary Medicine (D.V.M.) degree or Veterinary Medicine Doctorate (V.M.D.).

Staff veterinarians may be needed at any time for animal emergencies such as rescues or births. They are sometimes required to travel when transporting animals, or to monitor animals that are being released after they have been successfully rescued and rehabilitated.

Jim McBain, D.V.M.
Corporate Director, Veterinary Services
SeaWorld San Diego

1. *What's the most exciting part of your job?*
   My attraction to marine mammal medicine, especially cetaceans is the pioneering nature of the work. In relative terms, very little is known about marine mammals when compared to most terrestrial mammals.

2. *What do you want to get involved with next?*
   I'm still having fun with marine mammal medicine so I haven't thought about a change.

3. *What's your most unforgettable moment on the job?*
   My first killer whale birth was, hands down, the most unforgettable. The birth process in mammals has, in my book, always qualified as a miracle. The birth of a large cetacean is amazing. My most unforgettable experience was the 14-month rehabilitation of J.J. the gray whale. That experience may never be duplicated.

4. *What advice do you have for young people who would like to do what you do?*
   If you want a job like the one I have, don't be in a hurry. You must first focus on the necessary education then work on gaining the experience needed to qualify for the job of your dreams. Take pleasure in the process. If you feel a need to hurry and don't enjoy the journey, you probably will be disappointed when you reach what you thought was your dream job. If you have dreams, make sure they are realistic, then don't let go of them.

5. *What school subjects would be helpful for your field of work?*
   I have had many subjects that were easy for me and many that were difficult, but I have never taken any that weren't useful. You can't always judge at the time how a course is going to fit into your future.

6. *What are your favorite books related to your field of work?*
   When dealing with medicine, you must have a reference library and use it often. If you are to remain current in your profession you must also dedicate time to reading journal publications that are relevant to your chosen field of pursuit.

To begin a whale transport, animals like this killer whale are placed into a custom-made nylon stretcher before being lifted out by a crane.

Animal Transportation

Animals at Busch Gardens and SeaWorld rarely need to be moved. Animals may be moved, however, for breeding programs. Some successfully rehabilitated animals may be released as well.

SeaWorld's process of transporting whales and dolphins began in 1965 and is now called *Shamu Express*. To prepare a whale or dolphin for its trip, the water level in a holding area is lowered and the animal is placed in a custom-designed nylon stretcher. The stretcher is lowered into a water-tight, padded transport unit. The animals are immersed in water during their journey.

Once loaded in the transport units, the animals are driven to an airport--usually at night to take advantage of cooler temperatures and less traffic in the air and on the ground.

At the airport, the whales or dolphins are loaded into a chartered jet using cranes and specially designed cargo loaders. Throughout the course of travel, animal care specialists, trainers, and veterinarians watch and attend to the animals. Once the dolphins or whales have arrived at the destination, they are lowered into their pools using a crane and the specially designed stretcher. If they are being released, the animals are placed on boats and taken out to sea.

The water and transport units alone may weigh 11,340 kg (25,000 lb), and the total cargo load can be more than 68,000 kg (150,000 lb.).

Dolphins, sharks, and killer whales are moved by using the *Shamu Express* system. *Shamu Express* provides safe and comfortable travel for these animals, but it requires a great deal of planning and hard work.

Animal Research

A wide variety of information is gathered by researchers who study animals in zoological parks and in the wild. Observing an animal's diet, breeding behavior, and social interactions provides clues on how to meet all its needs in a zoological park. Studying animals in a zoological park is often the best and sometimes the only way to observe and record behaviors. Some of these studies would be difficult or impossible to do in the wild.

Animal researchers have dedicated their lives to animals, and these positions are highly sought after. Funding for animal research is limited, so positions may be difficult to find. What researchers learn at zoological parks plays an important role in creating and maintaining *Species Survival Plans* and setting criteria for preserving habitats and ecosystems.

Behaviorist

Behaviorists observe an animal's behavior. This may include breeding behaviors or how an animal responds to changes in its environment. Some observations can lead to a habitat design that is more comfortable for the animal. Other observations add to the success of breeding programs. For example, observing flamingos during their breeding season helps to understand what materials are needed to build their nests at zoological parks.

Some of the duties of a behaviorist include...

- conducting behavioral research studies
- maintaining accurate records
- distributing data to veterinarians, curators, animal care specialists, and the design and engineering department

Behaviorists usually have a Master's or Doctorate degree in psychology or biological sciences and a minimum of two years experience in field research and animal observation.

Behaviorists gather detailed animal information at SeaWorld and Busch Gardens. Here researchers study a mother and calf to learn more about the nursing behaviors of killer whales.

Todd Robeck, D.V.M., Ph.D.
Corporate Director of Theriogenology
SeaWorld San Antonio

1. *What's the most exciting part of your job?*
   My Ph.D. is in reproductive physiology.
   The most exciting part of my job is
   when all of the years of research with a
   particular species results in a calf being
   born. It's rewarding to know that what you have strived to
   accomplish for a long time can actually work.

2. *What do you want to get involved with next?*
   I have many goals yet to be accomplished with the various marine
   mammals in our collection. As with killer whales 15 years ago,
   very little is known about the basic reproduction of many of our
   species, and I would like to change that.

3. *What's your most unforgettable moment on the job?*
   The moment I knew Kasatka, one of the killer whales I work
   with, was pregnant. The next best moment was getting a call
   letting me know that she had successfully delivered her calf.

4. *What advice do you have for young people who would like to
   do what you do?*
   Students need to be willing to spend a lot of time in school. They
   should also enjoy the field they choose and not pick a field just
   to work with marine mammals. In my case, I would be very
   happy working with horses and cows. Thus, if I wasn't able to
   work with marine mammals, I would still get pleasure from
   my career.

5. *What school subjects would be helpful for your field of work?*
   I would recommend biology, physiology, animal behavior.
   These classes will help you understand living organisms and
   how animals interact with each other and their environment.

6. *What are your favorite books related to your field of work?*
   The Dolphin Doctor by Sam Ridgway is a great book. Wyland
   and Richard Ellis have some good books, but read as many
   books on marine mammals as possible.

Registrar

Registrars maintains extensive records on the animal collection. For this position, attention to detail is crucial. Registrars must stay current on all government rules and regulations regarding animal care and trade.

Some of their duties include...

- documenting births and deaths of animals
- maintaining studbooks
- handling paperwork associated with the loan or transfer of animals to other parks
- tracking offspring resulting from breeding loans

The minimum requirements for the registrar position is one year of experience with a computerized animal inventory and a Bachelor's degree in zoology or biological sciences. The registrar works with all of the animal services departments, curators, and government agencies connected to the welfare of animals in zoological parks.

Geneticist

Geneticists study an animal's DNA. Among other things, studying DNA can help determine how closely individual animals are related. This is especially helpful in animal breeding programs.

Some of their duties include...

- proposing and conducting research projects involving endangered species in the park and in the wild
- assisting in the development of breeding programs and *Species Survival Plans*
- keeping up to date with technology
- actively seeking research funds by writing grants and papers and by attending fundraiser events

Geneticists are required to have a Master's degree in molecular biology and genetics, as well as several years experience in genetic research for conservation of endangered species.

Research Biologist

Research biologists have a central position in a zoological park. Many departments depend on research biologists for reference updates and current animal information. Research biologists juggle many projects simultaneously, and are responsible for the financing, accuracy, and completion of those projects.

Some of their duties include...

- overseeing research projects
- overseeing technical publications and presentations
- designing and implementing research projects in the park and in the field
- overseeing corporate conservation projects with outside organizations
- making professional presentations at meetings
- serving on state and federal conservation committees

A research biologist needs to have a Ph.D. or Master's degree in biological sciences and many years work experience within the zoological community.

Research biologists study the life history of animals such as bottlenose dolphins (*Tursiops truncatus*) both in zoological facilities and in the wild.

Daniel K. Odell, Ph.D.
Research Biologist
Hubbs-SeaWorld Research Institute

1. *What's the most exciting part of your job?*
The variety. I never know what will be next: a whale stranding, a dolphin birth, or the opportunity to visit international colleagues.

2. *What do you want to get involved with next?*
This is always a difficult question because there are so many possibilities. There is always the need to write manuscripts and publish data. I'd like to investigate the underwater 'soundscape' in the estuarine waters of Florida on a year-round basis.

   Also, I'd like to use small, remotely piloted aircraft to study dolphin behavior.

3. *What's your most unforgettable moment on the job?*
A toss-up between meeting President Bush (the elder) and seeing a killer whale calf born.

4. *What advice do you have for young people who would like to do what you do?*
Develop a solid foundation in the biological sciences before focusing too heavily on a special field.

5. *What school subjects would be helpful for your field of work?*
All of the biological sciences, chemistry, physics, math (including statistics), foreign language, scientific writing and speaking, and computer science.

6. *What are your favorite books related to your field of work?*
Handbook of Marine Mammals volumes 1-6, Academic Press
Biology of Marine Mammals, Smithsonian Institution Press
Conservation of Marine Mammals, Smithsonian Institution Press
Sierra Club Handbook of Whales and Dolphins
Sierra Club Handbook of Seals and Sirenians
Manatees and Dugongs, Facts On File Publishers

Ann E. Bowles, Ph.D.
Senior Research Biologist
Hubbs-SeaWorld Research Institute

1. *What's the most exciting part of your job?*
   I love exploring the lives of animals in
   remote places. I also love finding out
   things that no one else knows. I guess
   I'd have to say that the most exciting part
   of my job is the thrill of discovery.

2. *What do you want to get involved with next?*
   I want to find out if we can use new non-invasive medical imaging
   technologies to learn about marine mammal perception (what they
   hear, how they see, and how they feel about those things). Maybe
   one day we'll be able to tell what they think about us...

3. *What's your most unforgettable moment on the job?*
   In the long-run, what I remember best are the moments when I
   have felt most connected with the living world. Like the day I
   saw my first sei whale at sea. Or the day a Mexican spotted owl
   answered my version of an owl call through half a mile of
   lichen-draped old-growth forest. I had to hold my breath and
   stand perfectly still before I could hear him clearly.

4. *What advice do you have for young people who would like to
   do what you do?*
   You have to come to this field with an obsessive love of animals
   and nature. The best way to get it is to spend a lot of time with
   animals, even if it's just turtles or fish, getting to know them as
   individuals, the way you would human friends.

5. *What school subjects would be helpful for your field of work?*
   My field is called bioacoustics, which means the study of animal
   sound perception and communication. I had to study the physics
   of sound, statistics, psychology, and behavioral ecology.

6. *What are your favorite books related to your field of work?*
   The Language Instinct by Stephen Pinker
   Dinosaur in a Haystack by Stephen Jay Gould
   Guns, Germs, and Steel by Jared Diamond
   Why Zebras Don't Get Ulcers by Robert Sapolsky
   Lads Before the Wind by Karen Pryor

Field Biologist

Field biologists document the results of wildlife research outside of a zoological park. In addition to designing and implementing studies and research projects, field biologists assist in creating conservation programs to protect species in the wild.

Some of their duties include...

- developing and carrying out field studies
- coordinating field work such as securing shelter, food, transportation, and water
- working with other researchers in the field
- publishing field work
- making professional presentations at meetings
- maintaining field equipment
- acquiring legal permits to conduct research
- inputting data into computer files

Field biologists may spend long hours (often weeks or months) in primitive living conditions. They are sometimes exposed to intense weather and potentially hazardous situations. Although field research has its moments of adventure, most days are spent doing routine paperwork or quiet observation.

For a field biologist, a Master's degree in biological sciences is required. It also helps to have many years work experience within the zoological community.

Research done in the field is rarely glamorous. It sometimes requires years of quiet observation of animals in rugged conditions.

*C*lydesdale Handler

With some 250 animals, Anheuser-Busch has the largest collection of Clydesdale horses in North America. Clydesdale handlers are responsible for the care, conditioning, and showing of these powerful horses.

Some of their duties include...

- preparing and distributing food
- training the horses to work as a team and to pull the Clydesdale hitch
- assisting with medical examinations
- taking the Clydesdales out to public events and parades
- keeping the animal habitats and show areas clean and safe
- observing animals and documenting their behavior
- keeping health and diet records
- exercising the horses daily
- answering guest questions and speaking to educational groups

Clydesdale handlers working for Anheuser-Busch must be at least 21 years of age. They have varied educational backgrounds, but they all must have extensive experience working with horses. The breed of horse is not as important as the length of experience caring for them.

College degrees in related fields are a plus. Public relations skills are also useful as Clydesdale handlers interact with the media and the public on a regular basis. In addition, Clydesdale handlers must have a Class A Commercial Driving License because all are required to drive eighteen-wheeler trucks and trailers to transport the horses from show to show around the country.

Clydesdale handlers at Busch Gardens and SeaWorld parks work closely with many departments such as marketing, public relations, park operations, education, entertainment, and veterinarians.

Displaying the Clydesdales for public shows and parades involves a unique set of challenges for the handlers. Handlers are responsible for the wagon and harnesses, which require hours of polishing and cleaning. The work is physically demanding—each Clydesdale harness weighs 59 kg (130 lb.) and handlers may walk an average of 11.25 km (7 miles) on parade routes per day.

An average day for a handler consists of heavy lifting and other hard, physical work. They must be able to lift 59 kg (130 lb.) bales of hay and work shifts that begin at 6 a.m. and end at 7:30 p.m.

Finally, although Clydesdales are generally gentle animals, they weigh approximately 907 kg (2,000 lb.). Safety is always maintained while working with such massive creatures.

Driving the Clydesdale hitch is an extremely demanding job. Very few people in the world have the endurance, wits, and sheer upper body strength needed to control a hitch of eight Clydesdale horses.

Other Careers Working with Animals

"It's important for SeaWorld, Busch Gardens, and Discovery Cove to play a leadership role. That's really our commitment to what we do in terms of educating the people, displaying the animals, and conservation research—it's all the pillars of what we do in our company."

Brad Andrews,
Vice President
Zoological
Operations
Discovery Cove,
SeaWorld, and
Busch Gardens

*E*ducation

Members of the education department provide guests and students with information about animals and plants in the park. Educators develop and present behind-the-scenes tours, classes, outreach programs, instructional field trips, and camp programs. The goal of the education department is to make each guest's visit a fun learning experience and to help the public understand and appreciate the earth and its diverse wildlife.

Zoo education programs combine the fun of learning with the thrill of seeing animals in an up-close and safe environment.

Educator

Educators have one of the more visible positions in a zoological park. The educator is often the first person guests approach with animal-related questions, so their knowledge of all the animals and habitats must be up to date.

Some of their duties include...

- narrating about animals at park attractions
- answering guest questions
- leading guided tours for park guests
- teaching camp programs
- providing educational activities at birthday parties and sleepovers

Educators should have three years experience working with the public in a service-oriented job, as well as public speaking experience. Educators also are required to take college coursework in biological sciences.

Instructor

Instructors research and develop programs and activities for day and resident camps, sleepovers, courses, educational shows, and outreach programs.

Some of their duties include...

- developing educational programs and shows
- creating curriculum and informational resources
- conducting group programs including teacher workshops and classes for all ages and abilities
- presenting at professional organization meetings and conferences

Instructors are required to have one to two years of teaching experience as well as a Bachelor's degree.

Instructors must be able to match course content and instructional techniques to teachers' and students' needs. And like all teachers, instructors in the education department must be able to readily adapt their programs on short notice.

Science Writer

Science writers use their writing, editing, and proofreading skills to create educational materials for the park.

Some of their duties include...

- researching, writing, and editing curriculum materials, information booklets, animal fact sheets, program brochures, and other educational materials
- overseeing projects from first draft to final production
- writing and creating ads for the education department
- assisting with the design of educational graphics
- developing copy for educational Web site pages

Science writers are required to have a Bachelor's degree in biological sciences and training in science and technical writing. They often work closely with outside contractors such as printers, so print production knowledge is helpful.

SeaWorld and Busch Gardens education departments assist with the development of Shamu TV— a free educational series offered to schools nationwide. For more information on Shamu TV, please visit *ShamuTV.com*

Jennifer Shorey

Educator
SeaWorld San Diego

1. *What's the most exciting part of your job?*
   The most exciting part of being in
   education is the opportunity to meet and
   talk with so many guests. I especially
   enjoy interacting with children and
   getting to teach them about the animals we have here.

2. *What do you want to get involved with next?*
   The next thing I would love to get involved with at SeaWorld
   would be the animal care department. As far back as I can
   remember, I have always wanted to work with marine animals
   and there is no better place than SeaWorld to work with
   these animals.

3. *What's your most unforgettable moment on the job?*
   So far my most unforgettable moment at work has been killer
   whale calf watches. One recent killer whale calf, born September
   2001, required around-the-clock observation, and educators were
   rotated into this duty. I never thought I would have the chance to
   help in research and be able to be so close to a killer whale calf.

4. *What advice do you have for young people who would like to
   do what you do?*
   I would suggest taking a public speaking class. Also know that
   if you work hard and put your mind to it, all things you ever
   want to do are possible.

5. *What school subjects would be helpful for your field of work?*
   The subjects that have been most helpful to me are speech,
   oceanography, and marine biology. Because of these classes,
   I can now better relate to guests and have more confidence in
   my knowledge about the oceans.

6. *What are your favorite books related to your field of work?*
   I don't really have any favorites, but I do enjoy reading
   about the work of Sylvia Earle--she's a real pioneer in the field
   of oceanography.

Internet Coordinator

Internet coordinators are responsible for the creation and coordination of the SeaWorld/Busch Gardens Animal Information Database (*SeaWorld.org* or *BuschGardens.org*), an educational resource containing more than 2,000 pages of information, video clips, sound bytes, and images.

Some of their duties include...

- updating and expanding site information
- designing new Web pages
- exploring new online technologies
- answering guest email questions
- working with all animal services departments from all parks, plus public relations departments and the corporate environmental communications department to ensure accurate and up-to-date information

The Internet coordinator needs to have a Bachelor's degree from an accredited college or university, with college-level science and computer coursework to be eligible for this position. Even with such qualifications, computer technology is ever-changing. The Internet coordinator is expected to participate in seminars and classes that deal with Internet technologies on a regular basis.

The Internet coordinator should have experience with both PC and Macintosh computer platforms, excellent proofreading and editing skills, be extremely detail-oriented, and have the ability to handle multiple projects with tight deadlines. The Internet coordinator may be required to travel to professional conferences and business meetings related to the Internet.

One of the most time-consuming duties facing the Internet coordinator is responding to the thousands of email messages sent to the site every year. The Internet coordinator is also in charge of the "Ask Shamu" team—a group of educational experts that respond to all animal-related email questions.

Scott Gass
Internet Coordinator
SeaWorld Orlando

1. *What's the most exciting part of your job?*
   I find the creative freedom given me to help our on-line guests discover and explore the wild world of animals extremely satisfying.

2. *What do you want to get involved with next?*
   As a living educational resource, the SeaWorld/Busch Gardens ANIMALS website (SWBG-Animals.org) is in a constant state of evolution. One of our most exciting areas of growth are the on-line expeditions through which we take our guests – virtually – to the wildest places on earth!

3. *What's your most unforgettable moment on the job?*
   The ongoing expansion of our coral reef coverage provided me the opportunity to film the annual coral spawn at the Florida Keys reef tract. The raspy exchange of air through my regulator, the bulk of the camera in my hands, and the background tension accompanying any night dive were all carried away in the other worldly grandeur of this mass-spawning event. It was like being caught in a topsy-turvy, living snowstorm--unbelievable!

4. *What advice do you have for young people who would like to do what you do?*
   Stay current in the realm of web design, write frequently, and study and experience the world's varied environments and the animals that reside within them.

5. *What school subjects would be helpful for your field of work?*
   The design and development of a zoo-centric site such as SeaWorld/Busch Gardens ANIMALS requires a synthesis of varied academic fields. Current coursework in web design and technique are immediately applicable. Additional studies in graphic design, journalism, and biology are extremely useful.

6. *What are your favorite books related to your field of work?*
   I make every effort to stay current in the fields of design and biology by reading established journals such as *Web Techniques*, *Science*, *Nature*, *National Geographic*, *Discover*, and *Cell*.

Education Department Career Ladder

Most people begin their career in the education department as an educator. With experience, educators can advance to other positions including leads, instructors, assistant supervisors, supervisors, education manager, and director of education.

The classrooms at SeaWorld and Busch Gardens are unlike any that students have visited before.

The education manager is responsible for implementing the department's long-range goals; overseeing the daily activities of all staff members; and coordinating the department's activities, programs, and projects. This individual must be qualified to teach all classes the department offers, from pre-kindergarten to college level. He or she is ensures that budgets are maintained.

The education manager is required to have a Bachelor's degree in biological sciences or education, plus two to three years of supervisory experience.

As head of the department, the director of education is ultimately responsible for developing the long-range goals of the department. The director of education must stay current on the needs, trends, and current issues affecting education. He or she might serve on *Species Survival Plan* committees or on the boards of education organizations.

The director of education has at least five years of supervisory experience, plus approximately ten years of experience in the education field. A Bachelor's degree in the biological sciences or education is required for this position.

Joy Wolf
Director of Education
SeaWorld San Diego

1. *What's the most exciting part of your job?*
   Seeing the thrill and excitement on the student's faces as they meet their first marine animal up-close. Plus, working every day with an excellent team of highly motivated educators.

2. *What do you want to get involved with next?*
   SeaWorld San Diego's Adventure Camp Center opened in July 2003. This educational venue provides limitless opportunities for collaborative programs with our local school districts. I look forward to sharing the excitement of SeaWorld programs with ever expanding audiences.

3. *What's your most unforgettable moment on the job?*
   Some of the most memorable I've had in my twenty-five years at SeaWorld include touching a gray whale, seeing a dolphin calf being born, and watching Baby Shamu being born.

4. *What advice do you have for young people who would like to do what you do?*
   Read, read, read... I can't emphasize reading enough. I spend much of my day reading. I keep current by reading scientific and teaching journals, as well as keeping tabs on Harry Potter.

5. *What school subjects would be helpful for your field of work?*
   To manage a diverse education department I would recommend a liberal arts background. Speech/communication courses along with management courses and an area of science that interests you. A teaching credential or training in informal education is also helpful.

6. *What are your favorite books related to your field of work?*
   The Holy Bible – New Revised Standard Version
   Mammals of the Sea by Dr. Sam Ridgway
   The Sierra Club Handbook of Whales and Dolphins by Stephen Leatherwood and Randall Reeves
   Field Guide to Birds of North America by National Geographic
   Who Moved My Cheese? by Spencer Johnson M.D.

Video/Photo Services

Large zoological facilities such as SeaWorld and Busch Gardens often employ their own staff of professional video editors, satellite technicians, and lighting and sound personnel. Together, this team documents the important moments that occur at SeaWorld and Busch Gardens on a daily basis. They also contribute to the production of *Shamu TV*—an Emmy award-winning series that is viewed by some 30 million students every broadcast.

Photographers and Videographers

At a moment's notice, park photographers and videographers may be called upon to film the birth of a killer whale or the release of a rehabilitated animal. Perhaps the most challenging part of being a photographer or videographer is the talent needed to "tell a story with a single shot."

Some of their duties include...

- capturing still images or video images of everything connected to the park
- maintaining and updating equipment
- keeping up with new technologies in photography and video editing
- participating in educational programs

Photographers and videographers should have a degree in photojournalism, telecommunications, or journalism. They also need to have strong people skills, because video/photo services is often involved with promotional events.

Senior Videographer Julio Lopez struggles through a Florida swamp to document the manatee rescued on page 28.

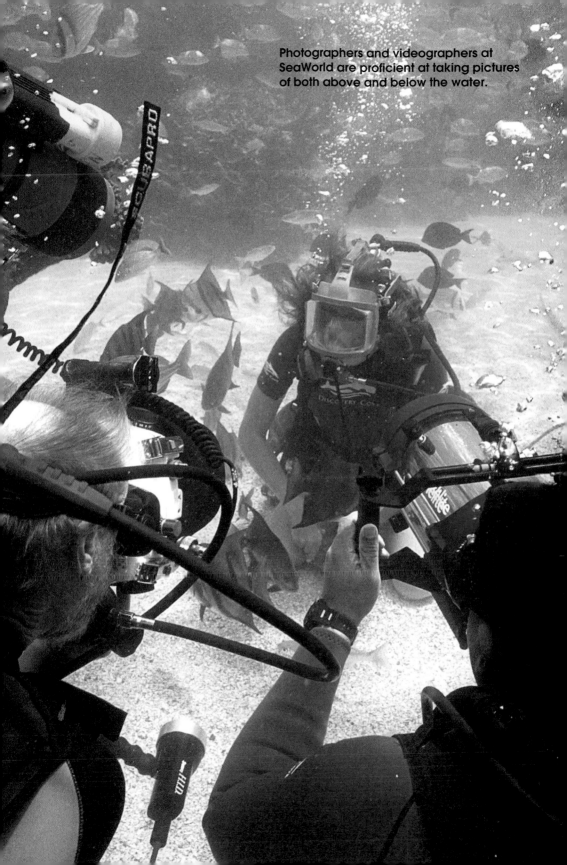

Photographers and videographers at SeaWorld are proficient at taking pictures of both above and below the water.

Laboratory Services

L aboratory services analyze samples taken from park animals. By checking tissue, blood, urine, and stool samples, they are able to identify parasites and other abnormalities. Water analysis is another important duty conducted by laboratory services staff.

Medical Technologist

Medical technologists primarily perform water testing and analysis of body fluids such as blood. They also maintain animal health records.

Some of their duties include...

- conducting tests and reporting test results
- dispensing vitamins, drugs, and other supplies
- maintaining laboratory equipment
- assisting in medical or surgical procedures

To qualify for this position, a person must be a registered Medical Technologist with the American Society of Clinical Pathologists (ASCP). Experience in a veterinarian's office is helpful. In some cases, an Animal Health Technician license is needed as well.

Laboratory Manager

Laboratory managers oversee work conducted in the lab. They have in-depth knowledge of laboratory equipment used by the staff.

Some of their duties include...

- conducting tests and reporting test results
- managing the dispersal of vitamins, drugs, and other supplies
- maintaining laboratory equipment and ordering supplies
- assisting in medical or surgical procedures
- training employees on safety and other procedures

Laboratory managers must be a registered Medical Technologist through the ASCP. They are also required to have a Bachelor's degree in biological sciences and five years clinical laboratory and supervisory experience.

SeaWorld and Busch Gardens laboratory staff analyze water and samples from animal physicals. Here, a medical technologist prepares culture disks to look for the presence of bacteria in water samples.

Pamela Thomas
Laboratory Manager
SeaWorld San Diego

1. *What's the most exciting part of your job?*
   The most exciting part of my job is
   the variety of experiences. Every day
   is different and usually the day I have
   planned is never the day that happens!
   I have the opportunity to work closely with the veterinarians,
   animal, bird and fish staff, and of course, all of the animals
   at SeaWorld.

2. *What do you want to get involved with next?*
   I want to continue to help get the word out about my profession.
   This is accomplished by speaking to student groups and
   professional organizations.

3. *What's your most unforgettable moment on the job?*
   The most unforgettable moment was probably being hired
   at SeaWorld. I am not a California native and could not
   imagine a job opportunity in my field of medical technology.
   The laboratory at SeaWorld is a top notch facility with
   state-of-the-art equipment. We provide excellent health care
   for the animals. Working here has been a career-defining event
   for me.

4. *What advice do you have for young people who would like to
   do what you do?*
   I would advise anyone interested in becoming a medical
   technologist to get a head start in math, chemistry, and science
   classes in high school or even middle school.

5. *What school subjects would be helpful for your field of work?*
   My degree is in bacteriology and public health. This type of
   background requires many classes in biology, bacteriology
   and chemistry.

6. *What are your favorite books related to your field of work?*
   The *Manual of Clinical Microbiology* has always been a big help
   to me. It provides a wealth of information when I am stumped
   over an identification of a bacterium.

A lthough the water quality staff does not have hands-on contact with animals, this team has a valuable indirect role in caring for animals.

Water Quality Technician

Clean, chemically balanced water at the right temperature is vital to maintaining healthy animals within an aquatic park. Water quality technicians perform tests around the clock to monitor water value.

Some of their duties include...

- monitoring and adjusting saltwater and freshwater systems
- performing chemical tests on water samples from all aquatic animals habitats
- adjusting water temperatures or water chemistry
- maintaining water quality equipment
- keeping accurate records

Water quality technicians should have a water chemistry background, computer skills, and a degree from an accredited institution in refrigeration, electricity, large bore engines, diesel mechanics, or engineering.

At SeaWorld, water is sampled and analyzed every three hours.

Early in the morning, food for the park animals is divided, weighed, and put on ice to keep it fresh for later use.

Food Preparation

Each animal at a zoological facility, whether it is a tiny sea star or a mighty Asian elephant (*Elephas maximus*), has its own unique diet to ensure maximum health for that creature.

Every day at SeaWorld, Busch Gardens, and Discovery Cove, some 3,175 kg (7,000 lb.) of high quality food is prepared for more than 65,000 park animals.

Needless to say, a large part of any animal keeper's day is spent preparing the diets of each animal under their care. For some employees, that means unloading truckloads of food brought into the park starting at 4 a.m. The food is then distributed to various locations throughout the park and is weighed and divided out for every animal.

Each bottlenose dolphin (*Tursiops truncatus*), for example, eats about 4% to 5% of its body weight in food every day, which generally equates to 5.5 to 11.5 kg (12–25 lb.) of food per dolphin.

The fish comes frozen to eliminate parasites and to allow the parks to store large quantities. Each day the necessary amount of fish is thawed out. Vitamins are placed into the gill slits of the fish to make the diet fully nutritional. The fish is weighed, placed in buckets, and kept on ice to keep the fish fresh.

The diets of birds varies depending on the species, so the aviculture department faces the challenge of preparing meals that may combine fish, krill, meat, insects, fruits, vegetables, or nectar.

Rescued animals also present their own challenges as some may be too sick or injured to eat on their own. Such animals may have to be tube-fed a gruel mixture until they are able to eat on their own. Young, orphaned mammals are bottle-fed specially prepared milk formulas.

Horticulture

The plants in a zoological park are more than decoration. They are carefully considered parts of animal habitats. The types of plants in and around each attraction gives visitors an idea of what the animals' natural habitat is like. The plants also provides a way for shy animals to seek out privacy.

Horticulturist

Horticulturists are responsible for the park's plant collection. A thorough knowledge of toxic plants is also important, because habitat plants may be eaten or chewed by the animals.

Some of their duties include...

- trimming, mowing, pruning and all other duties normally associated with landscaping
- weeding and routine maintenance on existing plant displays
- planning and creating new landscape elements
- keeping animal habitats, show areas, and guest areas clean and safe
- nuisance insect control

A horticulturist needs to have experience in landscape care and design, a thorough understanding of the park's geography and a strong landscaping background, including maintenance and design.

In order to maintain healthy displays, horticulturists must be constantly aware of environmental factors such as soil types, seasons, and sun exposure. The job can be physically demanding, and horticulturists often work outdoors during all types of weather conditions.

A well-landscaped animal habitat provides comfort and a potential extra food source to the animals.

David McElroy
Landscaping Manager
SeaWorld Orlando/Discovery Cove

1. *What's the most exciting part of your job?*
   There is always something new and
   different. At SeaWorld Orlando alone
   we plant some 1,250,000 annuals every
   year! It's exciting and challenging to
   keep the park looking beautiful while constantly fighting
   adverse weather.

2. *What do you want to get involved with next?*
   We are going to try our hand in formal English gardens. I feel
   this will be quite a challenge considering the adverse climate
   conditions here in Central Florida.

3. *What's your most unforgettable moment on the job?*
   It would have to be the time that I volunteered to go to the Shark
   Institute in Long Key, Florida. Once there we were asked to get in
   a holding area with the sharks in order to transport them to
   SeaWorld San Diego.

4. *What advice do you have for young people who would like to
   do what you do?*
   Stay in school, study hard, and keep your eyes open to
   opportunities that will come your way in the future. Gardening
   can be an enjoyable hobby, by the way! For some hands-on
   experience, get involved with gardening or landscaping projects
   at your home or school.

5. *What school subjects would be helpful for your field of work?*
   Landscaping, like engineering careers, requires knowledge of
   mathematics, which is necessary for calculating dimensions and
   layout of yards and gardens. Plant biology classes are great, as
   are courses in science, english, and even Latin, since many plant
   species are only known by their scientific name.

6. *What are your favorite books related to your field of work?*
   I try to read all of the great periodicals that come out describing
   the most recent and innovative ideas for landscaping.

California sea lions (*Zalophus californianus*) at SeaWorld's Pacific Point Preserve are displayed in a habitat that is both comfortable for the animals and visually appealing to guests.

Design and Engineering

I f you could build an exhibit for dolphins, what would it look like? The design and engineering department helps to create the unique animal attractions found at SeaWorld, Discovery Cove, and Busch Gardens.

Dolphin Cove at SeaWorld Orlando is an example of an amazing feat of engineering. This habitat contains more than two million liters (600,000 gallons) of water, a vast complex of water filters and chillers to constantly cool and clean the habitat, and a wave machine that simulates ocean waves. Many critical habitat components may not even be noticed by park guests. Details such as pathways, location of waste containers, landscaping elements, and even the number of stalls in nearby restrooms are planned by the design and engineering department.

Project Manager

Project managers create and develop exhibit plans while considering animal needs, human traffic flow, and keeper and animal safety. They weave these components together in aesthetically pleasing ways to create or redesign existing exhibits, show stadiums, and support facilities.

Some of their duties include...

- coordinating all of the physical pieces of a project such as architecture, painting, graphics, and signs
- developing project schedules
- overseeing project budgets
- working with contractors and key departments to ensure the project will meet the needs of the animals and park guests
- obtaining government permits as needed

The project manager is required to have five years experience as an architectural designer or an engineer with a construction management background, and a Bachelor's degree in architecture or engineering.

Gaining Experience

*"You will
love with
your heart
what you
see with
your eyes."*

**African
Proverb**

Starting at an Early Age

I n a 1995 Roper Poll, 87% of those polled agreed that zoological parks afforded them the only opportunity to see animals up close. If you or someone you know is thinking about a career working with animals, a trip to a local zoo may set in motion a lifelong commitment to this goal. This is certainly true for many of the trainers currently working at SeaWorld. The spark that led them to become trainers was first ignited when they saw humans and animals interacting together at a park show.

To begin a career caring for animals, be prepared to start with a voluntary or entry-level position. You can call your nearest zoo or aquatic park to ask for details on becoming a volunteer. You may also search the Internet for volunteer opportunities. Animal shelters, animal rehabilitation clinics, and some veterinary clinics welcome volunteers. Volunteer duties with an animal shelter or veterinary clinic will most likely involve working indirectly with animals (cleaning cages and preparing food). Volunteer duties at a zoo or aquatic park range from filing or answering phones to making educational presentations or feeding newly hatched birds.

Children can be exposed to animals through the adoption of pets or the building and maintenance of home aquariums.

Volunteering your time shows that you're serious about your commitment to animals. Develop a reputation for being an eager, cooperative, hard-working person, and your volunteer efforts may help you get a job in the future.

A trip to a local zoological park may lead a person to a lifetime career working with animals.

SeaWorld and Discovery Cove allow guests to become a "Trainer for a Day."

Gaining Experience

Looking for real experience working with or learning about animals? Children and adults alike can interact with animals in an up-close way at many zoological parks such as at SeaWorld, Busch Gardens, and Discovery Cove. A person seriously considering an animal-related career may want to participate in these fun and educational programs.

For example, guests can swim with dolphins and stingrays at Discovery Cove, or interact with sea lions, beluga whales, or dolphins at SeaWorld San Antonio and SeaWorld San Diego. Another very popular program at SeaWorld Orlando and SeaWorld San Diego allows guests to become a "Trainer for a Day." Participants ages 13 and up and in good physical shape get the rare chance to work side-by-side with a SeaWorld trainer for an entire work day through this amazing program.

SeaWorld/Busch Gardens Adventure Camps allow students to do a variety of hands-on activities such as weighing walruses, preparing penguin food, cleaning stingray habitats, feeding giraffes, and learning about zoological careers through a series of week-long camp classes. At SeaWorld and Busch Gardens Day Camps, children as young as preschool are given the opportunity to experience life at the finest marinelife parks in the world. Also, thousands of students spend the night at SeaWorld and Busch Gardens in sleepover programs.

Career Camp, operated out of the SeaWorld San Antonio Adventure Park, exposes people to all types of zoological jobs. Career Camp has produced more than 100 SeaWorld and Busch Gardens employees in many departments such as aviculture, animal care, aquarium, animal training, and education.

For more information on these interactive programs, please visit *BuschGardens.org*, *DiscoveryCove.com* and *SeaWorld.org*.

Options in High School

When you apply for a job working with animals, your prospective employer will assume you love animals. They will be much more interested in your education and experience. Are you serious about working with animals? The earlier you begin to pursue the right kind of education and experience, the better position you'll be in to secure the career of your dreams. A school counselor should be able to help students prepare to earn a degree in zoology, biology, chemistry, or psychology.

Zoos and aquariums often hire qualified people from within their own ranks. Those hopeful for an animal-related career may break into the field by taking a job in another department. Starting out in any department is a good way to gain park experience and knowledge. It allows you to establish yourself as a reliable and ambitious team member. This strategy may greatly increase your chances of working with animals in the future.

People who work with animals may assist in talking to groups, lecturing park guests, or performing in front of thousands of spectators at animal shows. Students may want to develop speaking skills in school by taking classes that involve speech, debate, or drama. Those who work with marine animals must

be in excellent physical shape because heavy lifting or exceptional swimming abilities are often needed. Participation in swimming courses, regular exercise, and a healthy, drug-free lifestyle will help to develop these valuable skills.

SeaWorld and Busch Gardens camp programs offers students a hands-on way to learn about the environment and animal-related careers.

Finally, many of the professional organizations listed in the *Informational Resources* section have special membership rates for nonprofessionals and students. People can learn more about animals and careers through these organizations' newsletters. Also, by attending local workshops and national conferences, a person might make some good contacts and get more information on how to chart a path towards a career working with animals.

*O*ptions in College

I f you're serious about attending college in order to pursue an animal-related career, consider the following questions:

- *Does the college have the program I need to prepare for my zoological career?*

- *How many people that graduate from the program find jobs in animal-related careers?*

- *Is there a zoological park, animal shelter, veterinary clinic, or pet store where I can volunteer or work while I attend school?*

- *Am I willing to move to take advantage of the educational and career opportunities this school offers?*

- *Are there internships available for working with animals?*

- *Who is teaching the courses—professors or graduate students?*

- *How much time do course instructors have to work with me?*

- *With the degree program I choose, what are some other career options if I can't find a job working with animals, or decide that I'm no longer interested in working with animals?*

College internships are available at many zoological facilities and allow college students to gain real life experiences. For example, SeaWorld Orlando's education department offers more than 40 paid internships. These internships are open to undergraduate students who have completed their sophomore year and are in good standing at a recognized academic institution. Applicants must be seeking a degree in education, science or recreation. Anyone interested in this internship should visit *SeaWorld.org* for more information.

Finally, some companies such as SeaWorld, Discovery Cove, and Busch Gardens offer programs that may reimburse a significant amount of college tuition for students who work for the park as a full- or part-time employee. Check with the human resources department of the SeaWorld, Discovery Cove, or Busch Gardens park near you for more details.

The following is a partial listing of schools and universities that offer programs that can help a student begin a zoological park career. Check with your school guidance counselor about other institutions.

Brigham Young University
Provo, UT 84602
(801) 378-3042
www.byu.edu
Animal health technology, Bachelor's of animal science

Colby Community College
1255 South Range
Colby, KS 67701
(785) 462-3984
www.colby.cc.ks.us:8000/
Veterinary technology program

Colorado Mountain College
Spring Valley Campus
3000 Co. Road 114
Glenwood Springs, CO 81601
(970) 945-7481
www.coloradomtn.edu/
Veterinary technology program

Emporia State University
1200 Commercial Street
Emporia, KS 66801
(877) GO-TO-ESU
www.emporia.edu
Programs emphasizing handling, care, and feeding of animals; internships at Emporia and Sedgwick County Zoos

Friends University of Wichita
Sedgwick County Zoo
Zoo Studies Programs
Friends University
2100 W. University Street
Wichita, KS 67213
(800) 794-6945
www.friends.edu/
B.S. and M.S. programs with emphasis in zoo science, zoo management, and zoo education; requires 360 hours of experience at Sedgwick County Zoo

Harcum Junior College
Bryn Mawr, PA 19010
(215) 525-4100 ext. 253
www.harcum.edu
Animal health technology; laboratory animal science; animal center management with a practicum at area zoos and wildlife facilities

Houston Community
College System
22 Waugh Drive
Houston, TX 77270-7849
(713) 718-5059
www.hccs.cc.tx.us
Animal health management; pet and laboratory animal management; ranch and exotic animal management

Humboldt State University
1 Harper Street
Arcata, CA 95521-8299
(707) 826-3011
www.humboldt.edu
B.S. and M.S. programs in aquarium sciences

Los Angeles Pierce College
Animal Health Technology Program
6201 Winnetka Ave.
Woodland Hills, CA 91371
(818) 347-0551
www.piercecollege.com
Animal health technology program

Michigan State University
Department of Fisheries & Wildlife
Natural Resources Building
East Lansing, MI 48824-1222
(517) 355-8332
www.msu.edu
Courses in zookeeping and aquarium management

Moorpark College Exotic Animal Training & Management
7075 Campus Road
Moorpark, CA 93021
(805) 378-1400
www.moorpark.cc.ca.us/
A.S. degree in exotic animal training and management

New Orleans Universities
Research Coordinator
Audubon Park Zoological Gardens
P.O. Box 4327
New Orleans, LA 70178
(888) 514-4275
www.uno.edu
Zoo research courses in anthropology, biology, and psychology

Quinnipiac College
Mt. Carmel Avenue
Hamden, CT 06518
(203) 228-5251
www.quinnipiac.edu
Laboratory animal technology program

San Diego Mesa College
7250 Mesa College Drive
San Diego, CA 92111
(619) 388-2600
http://intergate.sdmesa.sdccd.cc.ca.us/
Animal health technology program

Santa Fe Community College
Box 1530
3000 N.W. 83rd Street
Gainesville, FL 32611
(352) 395-5000
www.santafe.cc.fl.us/
A 74-credit hour program trains students in the vocation of zookeeper and other husbandry fields; also a four-year program is available in cooperation with State University of New York at Oswego.

University of Florida
College of Veterinary Medicine
Gainesville, FL 32611
(352) 392-3261
www.ufl.edu/
Program relating to the health of captive wild animals

University of Idaho
College of Forestry, Wildlife and Range Sciences
Moscow, ID 83843
(888) 8-UIDAHO
www.uidaho.edu/
Fish and wildlife courses with some orientation toward zookeeping

University of Illinois
Department of Ecology, Ethology and Evolution
Urbana, IL 61801
(217) 351-2224
www.uiuc.edu
Animal caretaker curriculum

University of Michigan
School of Natural Resources
Dana Building
430 E. University
Ann Arbor, MI 48109-1115
(734) 764-1817
www.umich.edu/
Zoo management and administration, landscape architecture

Wayne State University
College of Liberal Arts
Department of Biological Sciences
Detroit, MI 48202
(877) WSU-INFO
www.wayne.edu
Zoo management program; directed study courses at the Detroit Zoo

Informational Resources

For more information on careers working with animals, write to the following organizations:

American Association of Zookeepers
635 Gage Blvd.
Topeka, KS 66606

American Zoo and Aquarium Association
7077-D Old Georgetown Road
Bethesda, MD 20814

Bureau of Labor Statistics U.S. Department of Labor
Washington, DC 20212
Request *Occupational Outlook Handbook* (section "Environmental Scientists")

International Oceanographic Foundation
4600 Rickenbacker Causeway
Virginia Key
Miami, FL 33149
Request *Training and Careers in Marine Science*

National Marine Educators Association Publications Committee
P.O. Box 51215
Pacific Grove, CA 93950

National Marine Fisheries Service
3300 Whitehaven Street, NW
Washington, DC 20236

The Oceanographic Society
1755 Massachusetts Ave.,
NW #700
Washington, DC 20036-2102
Request *Careers in Oceanographic and Marine-related Fields*

Virginia Institute of Marine Science
Gloucester Point, VA 23062
Request *Aquatic Occupations and Ocean Opportunities. A Guide to What the Oceans Have to Offer*

White Pond Press
38 Litchfield Road
Londonderry, NH 03053
Request *Summer Opportunities in Marine and Environmental Sciences*

Glossary

aviculture – the care, housing, and feeding of birds.

biology – the study of life processes and living organisms.

CPR – cardiopulmonary resuscitation, the process of restoring normal breathing and heart beat after a victim suffers a cardiac arrest.

curator – an administrative director of a zoo, museum, or similar institution.

endangered – in danger of becoming extinct.

geneticist – a scientist who specializes in the study of how characteristics are passed from one generation to the next.

herpetology – the study of amphibians and reptiles.

horticulture – the art or science of growing plants such as fruits, vegetables, or flowers.

husbandry – the science and practice of breeding and caring for animals.

marine mammal – a mammal adapted to live in the marine environment and dependent on the ocean for food.

psychology – the study of how and why animals and humans do what they do.

scuba – Originally an acronym for Self Contained Underwater Breathing Apparatus; a portable compressed air apparatus used for breathing under water while swimming.

Species Survival Plan – a program for managing captive populations of certain threatened or endangered animals, administered by the American Zoo and Aquarium Association.

studbook – a comprehensive record of all births, deaths, and transfers of captive animals of a particular species.

threatened – likely to be in danger of becoming extinct.

Bibliography

Baldwin, R.F., "Doctoring the Exotic." *Sea Frontiers* 37 (1), 1991, pp. 30–35.

Byrum, Jody. *A World Beneath the Waves. Whales, Dolphins, and Porpoises.* San Diego: SeaWorld, Inc., 1998.

Careers in Oceanography and Marine-related Fields; a Special Edition with Emphasis on Opportunities for Sensory or Physically Disabled Persons. Washington, DC: The Oceanography Society, 1990.

Chase, V. "I'll do anything to work with whales or dolphins!" *Current,* 1992.

Dierauf, Leslie A., and F.M.C. Gulland, eds. *CRC Handbook of Marine Mammal Medicine, 2nd Edition.* Boca Raton, Florida: CRC Press, Inc. 2001.

Fox, W. *Conservation Career Closeup: National Marine Fisheries Service.* Charleston, New Hampshire: Earth Work, 1992.

Heitzman, Ray. *Opportunities in Marine and Maritime Careers, 2nd Edition.* Lincolnwood, Illinois: National Textbook Company, 1990.

Luoma, Jon R. *A Crowded Ark: The Role of Zoos in Wildlife Conservation.* Boston: Houghton Mifflin Co., 1987.

Miller, Louise. *Careers for Animal Lovers and other Zoological Types.* Lincolnwood, Illinois: National Textbook Company, 1991.

Nuzzolo, Debbie. *Dolphin Discovery. Bottlenose Dolphin Training and Interaction.* San Diego: SeaWorld, Inc., 1999.

Parham, Donna. *To the Rescue! The SeaWorld/Busch Gardens Animal Rescue and Rehabilitation Program.* San Diego: SeaWorld, Inc., 2001.

Ricciuti, Edward R. *They Work with Wildlife; Jobs for People Who Want to Work with Animals.* New York: Harper Collins Children's Books, 1983.

Ridgway, Sam H. *The Dolphin Doctor.* Second Edition. Dublin, New Hampshire: Yankee Publishing, 1995.

Robinson, Michael H. "Beyond the Zoo: The Biopark." *Defenders* 62 (6) 1987.

Shorto, R. *Careers for Animal Lovers.* Brookfield, Connecticut: The Millbrook Press, 1992.

Taylor, David. *Vet on the Wild Side: Further Adventures of a Wildlife Vet.* New York: St. Martin's Press, Inc., 1991.

Thomas, J. and D. K. Odell. *Strategies for Pursuing a Career in Marine Mammal Science.* The Society for Marine Mammalogy. *pegasus.cc.ucf.edu/~smm/strat.htm*

Virtue, Noel. *Among the Animals: A Zookeeper's Story.* Chester Springs, Pennsylvania: Dufour, 1989.

Western, David and Mary C. Pearl, eds. *Conservation for the Twenty-first Century.* New York: Oxford University Press, 1989.

Shamu TV®

So You Want to Work With Animals?, 1998

To Be or Not to Be a Vet, 2000

Wild Careers, 2001

Amazing Animal Rescues, 2001

Web Sites

Animal information from SeaWorld and Busch Gardens
SeaWorld.org
BuschGardens.org

The Alliance of Marine Parks and Aquariums
www-biology.ucsc.edu/alliance

American Zoo and Aquarium Association
www.aza.org

International Association for Aquatic Animal Medicine
www.iaaam.org

International Marine Animal Trainers Association
www.imata.org

Index

Goals of the SeaWorld and Busch Gardens Education Department

Based on a long-term commitment to education, SeaWorld and Busch Gardens strive to provide an enthusiastic, imaginative, and intellectually stimulating atmosphere to help students and guests develop a lifelong appreciation, understanding, and stewardship for our environment. Specifically, the goals are...

- To instill in students and guests of all ages an appreciation for science and a respect for all living creatures and habitats.
- To conserve our valuable natural resources by increasing awareness of the interrelationships of humans and the environment.
- To increase students' and guests' basic competencies in science, math, and other disciplines.
- To be an educational resource to the world.

"For in the end we will conserve only what we love. We will love only what we understand. We will understand only what we are taught." — B. Dioum

Want more information?

If you have questions about animals, call **1–800–25–SHAMU** (1-800-257-4268). TDD users call **1–800–TD–SHAMU** (1-800-837-4268). These toll-free phone numbers are answered by the SeaWorld Education Department.

SeaWorld and Busch Gardens have books, teacher guides, posters, and videos available on a variety of animals and topics. Call or write to request an Education Department Publications catalog or shop online at *swbg-estore.com*

Visit the SeaWorld/Busch Gardens Animal Information Database at *SeaWorld.org* or *BuschGardens.org*

Email us at *shamu@seaworld.org*

Anheuser-Busch Adventure Parks

SeaWorld Orlando
(800) 406–2244
7007 SeaWorld Dr.
Orlando, FL 32821

SeaWorld San Antonio
(210) 523–3606
10500 SeaWorld Dr.
San Antonio, TX 78251

SeaWorld San Diego
(800) 380–3202
500 SeaWorld Dr.
San Diego, CA 92109

Discovery Cove
(877) 4–DISCOVERY
6000 Discovery Cove Way
Orlando, FL 32821

Busch Gardens Tampa Bay
(813) 987–5555
P.O. Box 9158
Tampa, FL 33674-9158

Busch Gardens Williamsburg
(757) 253–3000
One Busch Gardens Boulevard
Williamsburg, VA 23187-8785